Catch Your

Breath

Tender Meditations
for Caregivers

Linda Spalla

BALBOA.
PRESS
A DIVISION OF HAY HOUSE

To my dear friend Liz-
Enjoy + share!
Linda
Christmas 2014

Balboa Press books may be ordered through booksellers or by contacting:

Balboa Press
A Division of Hay House
1663 Liberty Drive
Bloomington, IN 47403
www.balboapress.com
1 (877) 407-4847

Printed in the United States of America.

ISBN: 978-1-4525-2223-4 (sc)
ISBN: 978-1-4525-2225-8 (hc)
ISBN: 978-1-4525-2224-1 (e)

Library of Congress Control Number: 2014916502

Balboa Press rev. date: 10/17/2014

Contents

The Early Days

In the Throes of the Day to Day

Embracing Change

The End and the Beginning

Dedication

To my mother, the best person
I have ever known.

Acknowledgements

The quotations used at the start of each meditation were found from Internet searches on various sites, such as Pinterest, BrainyQuote.com, bartelby.com, Bartlett's Quotations, Thinkexist.com, and Goodreads.com. They are sourced exactly as they were on the Web sites.

Many thanks to my mother for giving me the opportunity to care for her in her last days and for providing the inspiration for *Catch Your Breath*. My daughter will be surprised to know that she was the secondary inspiration for the book, as it was written during a difficult time in her life when this mother's deep love could not solve her problems. I reached back to the tender relationship with my own mother to steady my frustration and hopefully give her a benchmark for embracing the mother-daughter relationship. Thank you, Natalie!

Many thanks to my readers (Sharon, Cindi, Jodi, Jane, and Beth) for investing your time in my work and for your tremendous support and positive comments. And most especially, I owe much gratitude to Jeanie Thompson, executive director of the Alabama Writers' Forum, for her professional insight and encouragement.

And finally, thanks to Bernie, who is my late-in-life gift.

There are only four kinds of people in the world:
those who have been caregivers;
those who currently are caregivers;
those who will be caregivers;
and those who will need caregivers.

—Rosalynn Carter

Alzheimer's Reading Room, Quote of the Day

Introduction

I had the dearest mother in the world. Southern to the core, gentle, gracious, and faithfully hospitable, she thus became a caregiver's dream when her sudden illness intruded into our lives. Even with mother's easy personality, I found myself overwhelmed by caregiving. It was constant, brutal, fulfilling, tender, sad, frustrating, relentless, and surprising, all rolled into one intimidating ball of commitment. My journey with caregiving lasted for eight months. I was a single woman, twice divorced, so the journey was doubly arduous.

This very mother taught me always to "do the right thing." And I did. I took care of her, loved her, met all of her needs, and gave it everything I had—and she knew it. I was not perfect. I said hurtful barbs I now regret; I fell into some ugly behavior I also regret. In the end, however, I had the overall satisfaction of knowing that I did indeed "do the right thing," and that has made all the difference in my memories.

Some of you have come by caregiving as a voluntary decision; others of you have been somewhat hijacked into it. Maybe there was no other choice because of your family or financial situation. Maybe your loved one chose you even when you were not a willing participant. I have to believe the latter situation would be the hardest. Regardless of how you entered the realm of caregiving, I hope these short and very honest meditations will provide you with solace, a dose of empathy, and daily courage. Take ten minutes each day to "catch your breath."

You may choose to read them day by day in succession as listed or by random topic, depending on where you are in the caregiving cycle. The sixty meditations represent eight months of caregiving, moving from my mother's diagnosis to her death, her funeral, and the aftermath of dealing with life once she was gone.

You will most likely laugh out loud in some sections and read through your tears in others. Catch your breath in the respite of a quiet moment and embrace that you are not alone.

The Early Days

Chapter 1

A Dose of Overconfidence

We must be willing to let go of the life we have
planned, so as to have the life that is waiting for us.

—Joseph Campbell, *The Power of Myth*

When I was in my midfifties, my dear mother, who was eighty years of age, suddenly found blood in her urine—copious amounts of blood. After a trip to the ER, we discovered that a great deal more was going on inside her body, which led to a diagnosis of advanced leukemia. Suddenly, in one long afternoon, our world turned upside down and the oncologist with a gentle demeanor conveyed to my mother that she had about thirty days to live. He recommended no chemotherapy because of her age and the rarity of the type of leukemia she had. He conveyed the diagnosis and the prognosis, smiled, patted her hand, and quietly left. I was stunned. Mother was devastated, and through tears she asked for her preacher to come to the hospital to talk with her about the courage to face death. No one knew what to say or think. Yesterday she was tucked away happily in an independent-living facility with an active social life and pleasant camaraderie; today she was dying!

All sorts of personnel came into my mother's hospital room that afternoon, including social workers asking if Mother wanted a nursing home, assisted-living facility, or hospice. With a surge of indignant confidence, I blatantly stated that we would have none of their services—I would take her home with me. I would provide the best thirty days she had ever had.

That afternoon's revelation, which was supposed to last thirty days, turned into eight months and led me to understand what it meant to live on fumes, a phenomenon understood by all caregivers. Though my initial burst of self-confidence was healthy, loving, and well-intentioned, it was not very realistic. Caregiving is like step-parenting. It's one of the single most difficult tasks you will ever perform. You don't embrace its ramifications until you get in the middle of it. What caregivers learn is that their gas tanks run low most of the time and day-to-day living is about surviving on the fumes. All of your gas is burned off so quickly that there's nothing left to fuel your soul or body. You give everything you have away. It's a lonely time, especially if, like me, you're single. It's a time for self-reflection and making sure your psyche is intact and secure. It's a time for venting to good friends and reading the Psalms in which David can relate to your heartaches and challenges. It's a time to draw on family to help you.

I was over-confident; I was sure I could do it. I sold that to my mother, and she believed in me. What I didn't know, and what no one knows, is truly how long the tending can last. Consider all the options carefully and push aside that rush to over-confidence. Think through a possible elongated period of tending and make sure you are truly up for it. Consider your finances and your support system, your own health, and your personal stamina. Consider the impact your tending will have on all of your other relationships inside your family and social network.

Would I do anything differently? Absolutely not—and neither would you, I suspect.

Chapter 2

Rearranging Space and Finding Some for You

This was the rearranged space of yesterday.
—**Deborah Levy,** *Swimming Home*

When you agree to take on the role of caregiver, your space is suddenly violated. There is an invasion of privacy that pushes the familiar routine of daily living and habits aside—for example, where and how people sit at the table for meals, where people watch television, where people sleep, and how they navigate through the interior of your house. Every resident will be affected.

A two-story house like mine meant that the only available bedroom on the main floor was the master, my bedroom. I rented a separate hospital bed and tried to remain sleeping in the same room as my mother, but she had many needs throughout the night and snored loudly. I realized that I had to move upstairs to a new, uncomfortable guest bedroom. The lighting was poor and the bathroom was inconvenient.

Suddenly I was redoing everything, trying to make a doable space for my life.

On the first floor, there were rugs to clear and furniture to move to make room for a walker and then eventually a wheelchair. I was glad to discover that most of my doors were wide enough for both walker and wheelchair and that I had an easy-entry shower. Never before had I thought of any of these elements.

Consider your living space very carefully before you accept a loved one. If you make the commitment, remember to keep the big picture before you. "Space is space" just like "things are things." The real dynamic is the relationship, the time, and the focus on your loved one. But in the meantime, a good night's sleep for you is a must! Carve out a cozy corner and be intensely kind to yourself, accepting that your usual space will be compromised for a time.

Chapter 3

A Bumpy Mattress
and Street Noise

Live simply so that others may simply live.
—Gandhi

M y new space upstairs was never comfortable for me, even though I tried hard to make it so. The bed's mattress was old and lumpy, and thus I didn't sleep quite right. The lighting was poor; the noise from the street—barking dogs, trucks, sirens, blowing wind—was intensified because of being on the top floor as opposed to snugly in the back of the house on the ground floor. I had never known all of this racket took place, and I became much more empathetic when my kids came to visit. I also noticed that the guest bathroom was ridiculously sparse. It had no Kleenex, no drinking cups, and no real warmth of accommodation. I quickly fixed that.

Even so, I still fell into the bed every night absolutely depleted, both mentally and physically. Almost every night I went to bed with wet eyelashes as the tears poured forth all the stress of the day and the awkwardness of a foreign space for sleeping. Wherever I had slept, however, the ultimate sense of aloneness would have most likely prevailed.

The interesting sidebar to using different personal living and sleeping space is how good it is for your visiting company. Sleeping in the bed they have to sleep in and using the bathroom they have to use is a good exercise in hospitality. Who knew? There are occasional surprising advantages which may result from being a caregiver!

Chapter 4

An Army and Dirty Carpets

We walk the plank with strangers.

—Sylvia Plath, *Channel Crossing*

*P*repare for the invasion. You will have all types of visitors: hospice nurses, social workers, sitters, home health-care workers, neighbors, ministers, friends, and family—some of whom you want and some you don't. Hopefully, unlike yours truly, you won't have white carpet! Yes, I had white Berber carpet throughout the bottom floor of my house. Slowly as the days passed, it became a dusty gray. The constant flow of traffic was unavoidable and essential, but I never grew accustomed to the unexpected ring of a doorbell and all of those strange people passing through my house.

Some of the army troops will be people you really, really like; others will be questionable. I suppose it just comes with the territory. My mother found some people in this support system a real boost to her day and disposition, so I tried to endure and smile. However, she could not stand one particular male hospice nurse. He tried so hard to be extra good to her, but something about a male nurse for a woman eighty-two years old was not generationally appropriate in my mother's mind. She was most uncomfortable with him. I had to agree with her about the wisdom of that assignment.

A sitter named Sally was my mother's mainstay. She was available for Mother throughout most of the day so that I could have something of a life. As time went on, Mother could not be left alone. One does have to buy groceries, go to doctors' appointments, and even have lunch with a friend. Sally was her confidante, and I'm quite sure she heard things I wished she hadn't. But c'est la vie. Mother needed a "best friend" during this time, and Sally became that for her.

Do your best to weed out the folks you really don't care for, and listen to your loved one. Try to make them happy. The army will be gone soon enough, and there will be a dull quietness.

Chapter 5

The Crystal Bell

The bell never rings of itself; unless someone handles or moves it, it is dumb.

—Plautus (Titus Maccius Plautus),
Trinummus **(IV, 2, 162)**

esting still on my grandmother's elegant, antique, marble-top table is my mother's little crystal bell. I ring it once in a while to remember the sound and to remember her. It is a beautiful cut-glass, crystal bell about six inches tall that shimmers in the sun's rays and rests proudly in the dim light of evening. It has a tall, graceful stem and commands to be handled with care by its mere design. During Mother's illness, it became my spine-tingler, my smile-bringer, my hair-pulling dread, my controller.

The bell was Mother's summoning method, suggested by me because it could be heard anywhere in my house. She would ring the bell when she was ready to get up, when she needed to go to the bathroom, when she wanted a change of venue, when she wanted something to eat or drink—for any reason. It was her lifeline to me or any of her sitters. Sometimes I hated that bell, especially at six in the morning! My sister used to say that she wanted to take that bell and hurl it out on the street. I understood.

At my mother's death I did not know whether to place it aside my treasures or smash it on the bathroom floor I had mopped and cleaned so often. Finally, after months of deliberation, I placed the bell among the rest of my bell collection to remind me of my mother's love and influence throughout my life. It was the right thing to do, but it took me awhile to hold it in fondness after it had held me in bondage.

Find a sure, reliable method of giving your loved one some control. The bell was very important to Mother, as it gave her a sense of authority over a piece of her life when everything else had disappeared. It was a symbol of dignity for her, of knowing her wishes and communicating them. It was such a small, simple object but with powerful significance.

What I would give now to hear Mother ring the bell one more time.

Chapter 6

A Cup of Hot Chocolate

We often need to lose sight of our priorities in order to see them.

—**John Irving,** *Trying to Save Piggy Sneed*

*C*aregiving produces a disproportionate view of almost everything. Small trifles are magnified and large issues that you know are important are somehow distorted or laid aside. Sometimes it just takes a second for your perspective to totally unravel. For example, take a simple cup of hot chocolate served up with great warmth and the anticipation of making your loved one feel better. Mother preferred a navy blue Ethan Allan recliner in my study where she spent most of her waking hours. She lost the use of her legs as time went on. This recliner was a roomy, comfortable chair where she could sit or recline for reading, television viewing, visiting with friends, and chatting with her sitters.

One morning when I was trying to do a good thing, I made Mother a cup of hot chocolate and served it to her in the blue chair. Almost immediately she turned the whole cup over onto herself, my chair, and of course, the white carpet! Hot anything on white carpet means a set-in stain. I struggle to write this because I absolutely lost it with her. It was an innocuous mishap that became the straw that broke my back that day. I screamed, scolded, berated, and tried to get the stain out of the carpet and the chair—neither of which were successful. Mother, of course, felt terrible, and I made her feel much worse. Just an extra moment of thought and restraint on my part could have changed this scene into something much more tender and forgiving. But not that day!

I'm not proud of that moment. You will have some moments like this no matter how hard you try. Forgive yourself. Realize that your nerves are frayed and the perspective gets warped. Move on because you don't have any choice. Tomorrow is another day, and hopefully a better day. Have a good cry, tell a friend what you did, and vow not to make the same mistake again. I never did.

Chapter 7

It's All About the Bathroom

> The first door in the hall leads to youth, the second
> door leads to middle age, and the third door leads
> to the bathroom.
>
> **—Jarod Kintz,** *This Book Has No Title*

*L*ife begins and ends much the same. Little babies are all about their poops. Dirty diapers, though aggravating, are a sign of good things happening inside their little systems. The elderly, and especially the elderly who are sick, experience a similar focus on bathroom issues.

Suddenly there are bedside toilets which have to be emptied all day long. Diapers reenter the picture all too often—and with that comes embarrassment for your loved one. Mother's resistance to wearing a diaper made things twice as hard for me. She could not get herself up at night and had to use the bathroom almost every hour. She refused to wear a diaper, saying that she couldn't stand to soil herself. Though my practical mind struggled with that, my heart understood. It was not in line with her genteel disposition and compromised her dignity. In reality, it gave me endless hours of extra work. It also forced me to hire expensive sitters and vacate my own bedroom. No amount of reasoning worked with her. Finally, I just had to let it go and offered her acceptance and understanding. It was a battle I wasn't going to win in the caregiving arena.

I spent hours and hours dealing with Mother's constipation. She would not drink water; it made her nauseated. Without fluid in her system, a good-working bowel was not going to happen. We tried everything—and I do mean everything. I learned to do things that nurses are trained to do, and so will you.

What can I say here that will make this better? There is not much, but I can emphasize the need to listen, empathize, reach out, and give a huge dose of understanding to your loved one. Issues like this make them miserable when they are already miserable enough.

To you as the meal planner and cook, I would suggest grams and grams of fiber, lots and lots of dark green veggies, beets, carrots, fruit, and water, water, water! Stay away from high carbs and processed sugar. Work together with your loved one, and I wish you better luck than I had.

Chapter 8

Gray Days

If months were marked by colors, November ...
would be colored gray.

—**Madeleine M. Kunin**

A s the days turned into weeks and weeks into months, we eventually reached November. I've never been a good November person because of the shorter amounts of daylight and, what I call, "gray days." Caring for Mother on these gray days was especially tough. I found out who I was and who I wasn't unfortunately—some of it was not pretty.

Fighting off depression was a deliberate choice. I tried to make myself remember that Mother was the one with the heaviest burden, not me. Nonetheless, I was greatly affected by the weather during this cycle. I even thought about buying a sunlamp for both of us. Maybe that wouldn't be such a bad idea!

We looked forward to college football on the weekends and took whatever advantage there was to go for rides on sunny days. Many times Mother never got out of the car. But just to be out was good. Company came less often on dreary days, and I felt less energized to cook and do other chores when the day had not been pleasant.

I'm not a creative person. I'm not a giddy, happy-go-lucky person. I'm not one to find humor in everything. I'm pretty much a dull, staid, predictable gal who takes life too seriously. I also have a bit of a martyr complex, a "look at all I've done for you" kind of thing! This is certainly not helpful in caregiving. So take it from me: try to laugh at more things, joke around, and be unpredictable and lighthearted instead of overwhelmed, burdened, and responsible. Make the opposite response to your usual, and see what happens!

As I look back, I sadly realize what I could have done on gray days. Mother loved to work with her hands, and I could have gotten her some simple craft kits. We could have played more Skipbo, her favorite card game. We could have worked jigsaw puzzles at the beginning. The television became her best friend, and thank goodness for that. It gave her hours of comfort.

Nowadays you can teach your loved one how to manage an iPad and bring the world to his or her fingertips. There are books to read, songs to listen to, and games to be played; there's even Facebook for chatting with friends. Don't make your loved one an invalid if they do not want to be! Good brains can still work even when the body is frail.

Chapter 9

Resentment and Feeling Trapped

Holding onto anger is like drinking poison and expecting the other person to die.

—Buddha

ome days you will wake up angry—angry at being caught in this caregiving cycle, angry at being trapped and unable to carry on with your normal activities, angry at being expected to navigate situations you have no desire to. We can all idealize that we are doing the right thing by caring for someone we love and making a great sacrifice for all the right reasons. But the truth is that it's hard, and once in a while, the anger boils to the surface. Personally, I think there would be something wrong with the person who didn't have this anger. If caregiving collides with an already difficult time in your life, anger and resentment will be intensified. I guarantee it.

Mother used to wonder why I was so angry, and as hard as I tried, I couldn't explain it to her with any degree of tenderness. It hurt her, I know, and that remains one of the pieces to this complex situation that I most regret. I tried very hard to hide it, but she was very perceptive. I wasn't angry at her as much as at the situation. And I had no one to blame but myself! She didn't ask to come live with me; I had insisted.

My best suggestion when you get angry is to take a brisk walk or go sit outside, away from your loved one. Get a breath of fresh air, go jump in the shower, make some brownies, or call a friend. Do a proactive "something" to shift your brain into a different gear. Do something besides feeling sorry for yourself. But more than anything, give yourself permission to be angry. Set about redirecting those angry feelings into some activity that is positive and creative.

I became angry very often, so I was constantly dealing with how to cope with those feelings. Maybe you will not be so bothered. We can hope.

Chapter 10

Next Comes the Guilt

There's no problem so awful, that you can't add some guilt to it and make it even worse.

—**Bill Watterson,** *The Complete Calvin and Hobbes*

After my feelings of anger came feelings of guilt, which occurred mostly because my mother was the ideal patient. She never complained about anything, never criticized me about anything, and never questioned anything. I know that she cried herself to sleep many nights because I could hear her weeping quietly. I know she woke up long before the 6:00 a.m. bell so as not to bother me any more than she had to. She had many moments of quiet desperation, but she endured them with grace every single day. I'm sure she missed my deceased father very much during this time. I'm sure she was scared of what death might bring. I'm sure she was saddened to be leaving her family and friends.

Every single night in my house—and I do mean every single night at bedtime—my mother caressed my face in both of her hands and said, "I love you, precious." Her point of view was simply one of gratitude. Her goal was not to be a bother. That intensified my guilt even more, and as time has moved on, I have discovered what a role model she was. I have and will continue to strive to be like her as I age. This, my friend, is one of the lessons that only caregiving can provide. Absorb this lesson well as you will someday become the role model for your loved ones.

In the
Throes of the
Day to Day

Chapter 11

The Gift

All I am, or hope to be, I owe to my angel mother.
—Abraham Lincoln

Though I have vowed never to move in with my kids, I don't know what the future will actually bring. If that day ever comes when I do move in with them, I have been given the perfect blueprint.

I will probably never have my mother's grace and gentleness. She inspires me every day. Had I not cared for her, I would never have received her greatest gift: that of an enduring, kind spirit amid such difficult times. She could have been bitter, ungrateful, demanding, or harsh. But she was none of these. She showed me how to age and how not to become a problem for her caregivers. Hindsight is truly twenty-twenty, and I so wish I had thanked her more for this gift.

I have spent hours perusing my mother's Bible and discovering her innermost cares and concerns. What a lesson that has been. I discovered a large manila envelope amongst her things, which contained all of the treasures from my childhood, even report cards from elementary school. I was always at the center of her world and her heart. I have some handkerchiefs which are hers, some trinkets, and some of her needlework. All of this is now precious to me, and I deliberately keep some article of hers in every room of my house.

On beautiful, blue-sky days when I'm walking, I look to the heavens and have all those conversations I should have had while she was living with me. I thank her for the gift of her spirit, which has left me better and stronger. She was indeed a light to the world and to me.

Chapter 12

Dance Lessons

I have come to believe that caring for myself is not self-indulgent. Caring for myself is an act of survival.

—Audre Lorde

You might be wondering what place a meditation about dance lessons has in this book. For me, they held top priority. I have always loved to dance and missed the opportunity to do so. I did some research and found a very good dance studio just down the street from me. Twice a week I had an hour lesson with a private instructor. Mother was safely with a sitter, and I could be home in about three minutes if she needed me.

There is no question that the dancing saved my soul. It made my heart sing. Not only did I move my body and get some great aerobic exercise, but it lifted my entire spirit. I felt unchained and free of the daily anxiety, interacting with activity that was artistic and creative. It also afforded me the opportunity to experience the touch of another human being. It sounds a little crazy perhaps to you, but it meant the world to me. Don't misunderstand—my instructor was happily married and his wife even taught at the studio. Dancing gave me a chance to be held and a sense of fitting in somewhere. Whirling around on the dance floor, light on my feet, brought back great memories of better days. Music has always been a huge part of my life, and the dancing just confirmed that. Whether it was a formal, staid waltz, or breezy swing, I absolutely loved it. I spent a fortune on this endeavor for over a year, and I don't regret it one iota.

Find something just for you that makes your heart sing! It might be gardening, photography, cooking, golf, or needlework. Find your comfort niche. It will make all the difference in your mental attitude. Give to yourself so you will have something besides fumes to give back.

Chapter 13

Sitter Stress

Sitting and waiting is one of the most miserable occupations known to man.

—**Diana Gabaldon,** *Dragonfly in Amber*

*E*very night at about 10:00 p.m., I would sit on my foyer stairway, looking out the front door and waiting on my overnight sitter. I lived on a cul-de-sac without much traffic, so I would patiently anticipate each set of headlights as they came into view. It became not only one of the loneliest times of my day but also one of the most worrisome. "What if they're late or don't show up? What will I do?" I would think. Sometimes they *were* late and sometimes they *didn't* show up. It was just part of the gig. It's one thing to be aggravated at nine o'clock in the morning; it's another entirely to face this kind of frustration at ten o'clock at night. The options were few.

Spend time researching all the senior sitter services in your area. Make the time for lengthy interviews with people who will potentially be in your home. Write down your list of important questions. Whether you let them see and talk with your loved one is a dicey call. My mother was alert enough, with all of her mental capacity intact, so sometimes I did let her sit in on the interview. So much was taken away from her that it was nice to give her some power in the decision. Mother, though very kind, was also very opinionated. There were some candidates she vehemently nixed!

I pretty much had around-the-clock sitters for Mother, especially toward the end. She lost all feeling in her legs due to the leukemia, and it required a great deal of pulling and lifting. You must have help if you live alone. And you must have help at night so you can get a good night's rest. Just when we would find a sitter Mother liked, something would change and that person would no longer be available. The best I can say is that you just have to keep working the process and dealing with the issues because they will never go away. There is no sitter who can stay twenty-four hours without a break, so be prepared to have two to three each day. At some point, after much observation, you just have to trust.

Today's technology has so many good options to protect your loved one and provide you with peace of mind. I would invest in all of them.

Chapter 14

Strangers in the Night

Fear makes strangers of people who would be friends.

—Shirley MacLaine

had only one major problem with a sitter. The study off my bedroom with the blue recliner was generally where the overnight sitter sat for the night. The television, which the sitter watched all night, was in that room, and Mother was right next door within easy earshot. My computer was also in the same room, and that became the center of controversy.

I shut my computer down each night and booted it back up the following morning. Early one morning I went in to turn the system on and found it already up and running. I knew for a fact that I had shut it down the previous night. The sitter had used my computer overnight without my permission! When I asked her about it, she lied to me and said that she had not. I knew better and reported my dissatisfaction (not accusation because I didn't see it happen), and I never used her again.

Be alert and aware when you have strangers in your house; truly anything can happen, and it's absolutely okay to be a little suspicious. But when you find a really good sitter, stroke them mightily with special little gifts and thoughtful gestures. A little on your part goes a long way. Just realize that sitting for the sick and elderly can be a boring, thankless, unpleasant job.

The best overnight sitter we ever had was an older African American lady named Elizabeth. She was kind, strong, and patient. Mother really liked her, and knowing this meant a good night's sleep for me!

Sitters can make or break your spirit, so spend time finding good ones!

Chapter 15

A Neighbor and a Rose

Little by little, a little becomes a lot.

—Tanzanian proverb

*N*ever doubt that little things can make a magical difference in the caregiving world. I had a wonderful neighbor who left a rose on my doorstep each morning for Mother. It became the highlight of Mother's day to receive this gift—so simple yet so lovely.

This gesture represented the spirit of my neighbor and also the spirit of my mother. It was the perfect symbol. For me it said that someone cared about what was happening inside my house. It said, "Hang in there," "I love you," and "See the beauty and not the pain." The rose, sometimes red, sometimes yellow, sometimes pink, was a statement of empathy. It was something to count on, to look forward to, evoking a smile even on gray days.

I hated when rose-blooming season was finally over. The rose was Mother's favorite flower. Who would have guessed it?

Thank God for kind neighbors and the simplicity of their love and care. We can all take a lesson here and remember to share a small daily gesture with those who are caught in the web of caregiving.

Chapter 16

Sibling Confusion

Start where you are,
use what you have,
do what you can.

—**Arthur Ashe**

*C*aregiving is the ultimate test for all involved, and no strain is potentially as great as that with a sibling. I had only one sister, and she lived an hour's distance from me. She absolutely did her part and came to be with Mother at least two days a week. Over the course of eight months, she surely spent a fortune on gasoline.

My sister was, on the one hand, glad that I had taken Mother in; but on the other hand, I suspected it made her feel guilty. She was quite open about the fact that she couldn't handle having Mother in her home, so it was either a nursing home or my home.

There was always that edge of tension on who had the final say about major decisions. I decided early on since I was the primary caregiver that I would give my sister the control of taking care of Mother's finances. She and her banker husband did a fantastic job with that and saved me hours of extra work.

Figure out a positive way to split the workload with siblings and say lots of prayers. Every old resentment and/or jealousy from the past will creep into the picture, and you'll find emotional baggage at the strangest crossroads. When I could no longer physically care for Mother and decided that I needed to put her in assisted living near me, I wrote my sister a letter. Somehow that infuriated her, and she whined to her own kids that I didn't consult with her. It created a wedge between us from which, until her dying day, we never recuperated—how truly sad.

Work hard with your siblings even if some counseling is required. However, don't expect it all to be perfect. Life is what it is, and sibling rivalry lasts until the bitter end. Don't let it get you down; do the best you can.

Chapter 17

Detours

A truly happy person is one who can enjoy the scenery on a detour.

—Author Unknown

*C*aregiving is a detour. It's often an unexpected turn down an unfamiliar route. We grow accustomed to going our usual and comfortable ways. Then suddenly a big arrow appears, and we fumble mentally to change our route or perhaps recalculate our internal GPS. If we had big plans, the detour will throw us off schedule and off balance. We tense up and resent the deviation and intrusion. It will surely make us late and arrive frazzled. If we aren't in a big hurry, a detour can be a delightful experience making us wonder why we hadn't noticed certain landmarks along the way before.

Living with the detours on a daily basis is hard. I am a walker, and I love the quiet time I spend in prayer and meditation as I walk my daily two miles. I tried to do that with Mother before I engaged sitters. I bought some long-distance walkie-talkies (this was 2001) and tried to teach her how to use them. I would get perhaps a block down my street, and suddenly Mother would call me. She would be frantic about something or in need of a bathroom break, even though we had just taken care of that. I think she became upset out of the fear of being left alone and knowing that I was not within earshot of that bell! It was probably also a little about being in control of something when most elements of life had slipped beyond her means of influence. Perhaps it was unrealistic of me to think I could squeeze in a daily walk. I finally gave up, realizing the detour was going to be around for a while.

The usual patterns must give way to a whole new set of lifestyle practices. Just accept the temporary detour. Embrace the new route; there will be some potholes along the way, without question, but there will be some life-changing vistas as well.

Chapter 18

Wheelchairs and Walkers

I can't bear the thought of my mother having to push me around in a wheelchair. I'd rather die quickly.

—Felix Baumgartner

I don't know about you, but I had never used a walker or a wheelchair before I began my caregiving journey. I had absolutely no appreciation for what their use meant in my home, in my car, to my physical body, or to the arrangement of my furnishings. If you are thinking of taking on the journey of caring for a loved one, I would encourage you to go rent a walker and small wheelchair for a week. It will be money well spent. Use it yourself and discover how encumbered the pathways are through your house.

See how you can't fit the walker through this door or that door, or how you must move that planter or push that favorite chair out of the way. Discover the difficulty in using the toilet or getting into a shower. Don't forget that small rugs can be a real problem for walkers and wheelchairs. All of those must be removed. Then there's your car. Lug both in and out of your trunk. Put a heavy object in the wheelchair, and try pushing it around streets with curbs or up a hilly sidewalk. Every movement will be a revelation. It is better to assess all of this prior to than during your caregiving experience. It will keep your loved one from feeling like such a burden.

And then ... prepare ... for ... everything ... to ... slow ... down. It takes time to use either a walker or a wheelchair. Your world will suddenly move in slow motion, and if you're a bit feisty like me, this will surely drive you crazy. I remember one day early on when I had tried to take Mother to a restaurant for lunch; it took her ten minutes to get from the car with her walker to the front door of the eating establishment. Nothing is simple and patience is the paramount skill here. Some days I had none!

Walkers should come with affixed baskets so your loved one can have easy access to items that they need, e.g., pens, puzzle books, a cell phone, Kleenex, the television remote, chewing gum, etc. It will save you many steps—trust me! Wheelchairs should be as light as possible or you will truly break your back. Spend time visiting medical equipment stores in your area and ask lots of questions about design, price, their return policy and the ability to rent versus purchase.

Chapter 19

Oh, My Aching Back

I can bear any pain as long as it has meaning.

—Haruki Murakami

I don't believe there's any way to avoid some back pain while acting as a caregiver. You are lifting, pulling, and pushing day in and day out. If you're single, the problem will be intensified. Here are some easy, practical steps to hopefully protect that back of yours.

Research some good back stretches on the Internet that you can do every morning or evening. Stretching is amazing therapy. Not having to leave your home will be so convenient.

Find a good chiropractor, massage therapist, or physical therapist who can keep your muscles loose and relaxed. Sometimes, insurance will pay, and sometimes not. It is money well spent.

Get with a nurse in the family or in your circle of friends, and let them show you exactly how to lift your loved one out of a chair, out of a bed, or after a fall. There are precise ways to do it correctly.

Check out your mattress and make sure it's a good one, not too soft or lumpy. Since you're possibly sleeping on a different bed, this is priority one! Maybe it's time to purchase a new one. Nothing will save you like a comfortable night's sleep!

If your back is in pain, who's going to help your loved one? Medicine is not the answer, as it often has side effects which might cause worse problems all around. Take control, be smart, and baby your back!

Chapter 20

Keeping Up with Medicine

Always laugh when you can. It is cheap medicine.

—Lord Byron

Okay, admit it—you have laughed at those medicine pillboxes. I'm talking about the ones which have daily dividers so that you can count out each day's dosage. I used to laugh at them too until I became a caregiver. Medicine becomes a part of your life, and keeping up with what, when, "did you or did you not take it?" will drive you crazy. If you find yourself getting confused, imagine how your loved one feels. Everything about their life has been disarranged, and they certainly should not be expected to keep up with their medication. No scolding!

It is part of your caregiver role to help them with daily medication. A spoonful of sugar truly can help the medicine go down, so try to keep it light and funny when it comes to all the pills. There will be a pill to sleep, to pee, not to pee, to poop, to soften the poop, to chill, to take the edge off pain; there will be blood pressure pills, an aspirin a day, and sometimes a vitamin or calcium. The list goes on and on—you'll feel like a pharmacy tech.

Every Monday I let Mother help me put her pills in each day's pillbox slot for the entire week. This gave her some sense of authority over her own life, though she hated taking any medicine. She did it under my watchful eye because it was easy to get confused. There was never any question after Monday's pill-counting exercise was completed as to what and when things went down the windpipe.

Just an interesting aside: Mother took a strong sleeping pill every night but still got up *every* hour to use the bathroom. Medicine is not an end to all of your problems! So much is aggravated because your loved one can't get a normal amount of exercise, which causes bodily functions to slow down. Many times you just have a big, fat catch-22, an unworkable problem. Suck it up and get through it since there's no other option. Just when you want to explode or break into tears, try bursting out laughing!

Chapter 21

Becoming the Parent

It takes a long time to become young.

—**Pablo Picasso**

I remember precisely the first time when I become the parent and Mother, the child. She wouldn't eat or drink, and I had to really bear down on her just as she had done to me when I was a child. It's a heart-wrenching moment that makes you want to leave the room and sob. I did.

My mother was a wonderful parent all of her life. She had always been a steady force, a great role model, a person of high moral character with good habits and good mental health. Now she was looking to me for all of those strengths. Suddenly I wanted to push back and say, "No, this is not my job. It's your job! Why do I have to be the parent?"

But I didn't say those comments, and you will not either. You will do what you have to do. Your best self is down inside, regardless of how you may feel about your loved one. You will rise above everything and your basic love will come through. The pressure to be that steady force creates immense tension.

I don't make light of it, but I do believe that you would not be reading this book if you didn't want to be the best you can be.

God help you if you have an ungrateful parent who is not kind to you. I can write easy words about that because I didn't experience it. Draw tough, consistent boundaries and decide how much and how long you can effectively get by. Make loving and good decisions with the advice of other family members, friends, and your minister. Brace yourself for guilt and possible criticism, but don't take it on. That's a dirty trick that you don't have to acknowledge.

Chapter 22

Praying

Go where your best prayers take you.

—Frederick Buechner

*I*f you generally don't pray every day, now's a good time to start. Mother had a daily devotion at the breakfast table, reading her copy of *The Upper Room* as she had done all of her life. How I wish now that I had made time to sit down and join her, but I didn't. We didn't choose to talk or pray together regarding spiritual matters. I see now that it could have been so revealing and so helpful for both of us. Mother never invited me into her devotional time, and I suspect she didn't because she was a shy, very private person and may have feared rejection. Even sadder is that I never invited her into mine.

My prayer time was typically during my daily walks, which were most often thwarted so I found myself growing spiritually barren. How stupid of me to allow that to happen. It seems so obvious now to me that I made a grave error here. Sometimes we can't see that which would help us the most. Mother and I could have spent every morning together at the breakfast table and fed both of our souls—oh, the missed opportunities which you realize you could have done so differently!

I recommend that you find what's called a prayer rock for both yourself and your loved one. It's a small, smooth stone with a cross or iconic symbol etched in the center of it. Something tangible to rub as you pray is a soothing exercise and also a daily reminder that you need to have some quiet time. The stones are less than five dollars and can be found off the Internet or from your church or other religious institution.

I also recommend the Book of Psalms, reading one Psalm a day. No one knew struggle, hardship, and challenge like David. His poetry is wonderful. I also recommend the book *Simple Abundance* by Sarah ban Breathnach. It's especially for women who are on a journey of self-discovery. It's a perfect match for caregiving days.

Chapter 23

Listening

When people talk, listen completely. Most people never listen.

—Ernest Hemingway

It took having a stranger in my house to drive home the point that I wasn't really listening to my mother. Her favorite sitter filled that role. Mother adored her time with Sally, and I often found myself a little jealous of their relationship. They would talk and talk and talk, giggling like mischievous school girls. Sometimes they would talk in whispers about the stuff of broken hearts and frustration, and maybe even about me. It happens so often, doesn't it, with families? We hear all of their comments, sagas, gripes, struggles, and pleas, but we don't really listen. It takes another person from outside the circle to satisfy that need. (It isn't surprising that I face this same dilemma with my adult daughter. She will say to me, "Mother, you're not listening.")

This mistake, more than any other, haunts me in my post-caregiving life. Mother needed me to really listen and understand. I spent my time trying to "fix" everything because I'm a fixer. That inadvertently added to her stress and mine because in reality, no matter what I did, I couldn't fix leukemia. All she really wanted was for me to hold her frail hand and listen with my love and empathy.

Learn this lesson early on and don't waste precious time like I did. It's a regret that I'm not proud to share. Forego fixing and just listen!

Chapter 24

Writing Your Way Through It

Give sorrow words; the grief that does not speak
whispers the o'er-fraught heart and bids it break.

—William Shakespeare, *Macbeth*

lease try your hand at a daily journal. It can be something so honest, so brutal, so touching that it might amaze you. You are safe because no other eyes will probably ever see it. It can be the window to your soul with nothing held back. You can write at night before bed (my preference), first thing in the morning, or during your loved one's afternoon nap. You will find that even if you've never considered yourself a writer, you'll have much to say!

Don't write in front of your loved one, as they will most certainly ask to see what you're writing. Do it in private and protect your inner sanctum.

I wrote 365 poems and a short story while Mother lived with me. It saved my soul. In other difficult times, I have written in a gratitude journal, making a list of at least five things I was grateful for each day. Sometimes it was hard to come up with five! What a great exercise to stay on the upper side of sanity.

You could write to yourself, directly to your loved one, to your siblings, to friends who don't seem to understand where you are, or to God. You can shout with anger or joy; you can scream or sob; you can go on a tirade; you can be your own counselor and sort out an issue. If you really, really don't want the words to ever be found, write and rip. Tear up the page. The writing was the release. I personally enjoyed going back weeks later and reflecting on what I had written.

There are few guarantees in this little book, but I absolutely guarantee that this exercise will be good for you. So write!

Here are some more poignant quotes to relish about writing:

> "Writing comes more easily if you have something to say." ˜Sholem Asch

> "If I don't write to empty my mind, I go mad." ˜Lord Byron

> "You must stay drunk on writing so reality cannot destroy you." ˜Ray Bradbury

> "Fill your paper with the breathings of your heart." ˜William Wordsworth

Chapter 25

Stay Near the Sun

Keep your face to the sun and you will never see
the shadows.

—**Helen Keller**

Regardless of the time of year, try to keep your loved one in the sunshine as much as possible. Do you remember the wonderful book, *The Secret Garden*, by Frances Hodgson Burnett? It tells the story of a young lad who had been turned into an invalid, sheltered, and bedridden. Suddenly a new friend arrives and thrusts him outside into the light, warmth, and beauty of the garden. If you haven't ever read this book, now would be a perfect time.

In the warm weather, get your loved one into that wheel chair and go for short walks, or just position them on a porch or in your yard, soaking up the sunshine. Not only will it lift their spirits, but it will also give them big doses of vitamin D, which will improve their overall health. If it's cold, find a morning sun window so the warmth bleeds through, or put them in the car and let the warm sunshine penetrate through the windshield. A lot of trouble, you say? Yes, but the therapeutic value will be tremendous for both of you!

Gray days are the challenge, but we've already addressed those. Create your own internal sunshine and wait for a better weather day.

Chapter 26

A Word About Hospice

Hospice means end-of-life care. The admission
ticket is a diagnosis from a doctor that you have
six months or less to live.

−Eleanor Clift

*E*ventually you will need help. Investigate all of your
resources and don't overlook using your local, not-
for-profit Hospice Association.

In my community there were a world of hospice
volunteers who sometimes came by just to say hello or
even to sit with Mother. If money is an issue for you or you
don't want to go the contract sitter route, this could be an
option. Certainly it's not to be taken advantage of, but once
in a while, the volunteer assistance can be critical. Hospice
provides nurses, social workers, home health aides, and even
massage therapists who can bring a soothing experience for
your loved one. Human touch is a powerful tool. I have a
dear friend who is a licensed, orthopedic massage therapist,
but she is also a minister in her own way by working with
hospice patients for no fee. Her spirit is so kind and her touch

so gentle that her patients love to see her coming. Her role, as with all of hospice, is not to heal but to soothe and reduce pain and stress.

When you have finished your caregiving journey, don't forget to make a donation to your hospice of choice. (By the way, schedule your own massage and treat yourself to an hour of relaxation!)

Chapter 27

A Dove's Nest

Mama Dove

She's gone now,
that mama dove;
dapple-dressed in taupe and gray,
nesting above me, beside me,
in weeks of gestating suspension.

My patio companion sans any others.

With black beady eyes,
she watched me calmly,
learning my moves,
unafraid, trusting of my
intrusion on her breeding ground.

I miss her presence!
God's simple assurance
of the promise of new life.

—Linda Spalla

T inherited a dove's nest on my patio when I bought my house. It was a teal green basket, rounded on one side and flat on the other, so as to fit snugly against the outside brick wall. For fifteen years I watched in the late spring and early summer as five or six sets of baby doves were born. The nest became piled higher and higher with twigs and leaves as each year more and more birds came to roost. Were they the same birds? There's no way to tell since all doves have exactly the same markings. But it was their tradition to return to this spot every year! It was a treat for my grandchildren and for me.

There is so much more to the story, however. Did you know that doves mate for life? Did you know that the mother and father birds take turns building the nest, sitting on the eggs, and then feeding the babies? They usually have only two or three babies at a time. I have actually witnessed at just the right moment in time when the mother lifted her wings and, rising up, dropped her eggs into the nest. I have witnessed at just the right moment in time when an egg cracked open and a baby dove appeared. I have witnessed at just the right moment when the mom or dad flew up with a worm and with vigorous oral thrusts fed the babies, beak to beak. These precise moments were rare, but I never forgot the marvelous sense of witnessing something just short of a miracle. After about five days, the mother dove gently lured the babies to fly out of the nest, sometimes landing safely and sometimes not. It was a scary session to watch.

For me and for my mother, the doves were reliable companions in a frenzy of unexpected ups and downs. They were a hitching post, something to hang onto and be inspired by.

Find a dove's nest or something similar to remind you of nature's dependable charm.

Chapter 28

You Are Stronger
Than You Think

I know God won't give me anything I can't handle.
I just wish he didn't trust me so much.

—**Mother Teresa**

On some days we want nothing to do with this wonderful thought from Mother Teresa. It is truly profound. Read it again. As frustrated as we may become, think of the magnitude of being trusted enough by God to endure, survive, and perhaps even thrive in your present circumstances. Caregiving is a time for strength of mind, body, and spirit. It is not for the wimpy! People who are caregivers have broad shoulders, big hearts, good self-esteem, and the ability to draw boundaries to protect themselves. Otherwise they quit, fail, or have a nervous breakdown. You would not be reading this if you were any of those people. So give yourself a well-deserved pat on the back and realize your own strength.

But you say, "I'm tired. I'm overwhelmed. I can't do it anymore." Maybe you're right. Today you are spent, but tomorrow you can. Tomorrow you will be blessed with more inner strength of mind, body, and spirit. Find a way to shift your perspective. Write in your gratitude journal. Look for those five things each day for which you are grateful. The more you look, the more you will find!

My former mother-in-law loved to say that if all your neighbors put all of their daily woes and cares into bushel baskets and lined them up at the street, they would decide to bring their own baskets back home. Why? They would see that their own life "stuff" would prove to be easier than their neighbors'.

Stay focused on the positive. If you bought this book, you've got disposable income. You've got two good eyes. You've got a good mind. You know how to read. And you have food on the table to give you the stamina to make time for reading. Get the picture? There are folks in this world who can't even get a drink of clean water much less take a shower, wash clothes, or cook. Some of them are caregivers! Imagine that and then be strong.

Chapter 29

Filling Up Your Gas Tank

> You can find inspiration in everything. And if you
> can't, look again.
>
> —**Paul Smith,** *You Can Find Inspiration in*
> *Everything. And If You Can't Look Again*

When we're hungry, we eat. When the car is low on gas, we fill it up. When the pantry is empty, we go to the grocery store. When there's no cash in our wallets, we head for the ATM. These are such obvious tasks that we hardly give them a thought. But when our souls are empty, we usually do nothing! Shame on us. You cannot live on fumes any more than your car can. You can pretend to be Superwoman or Superman, but you'll fall out of the sky pretty soon.

Identify the inspirational reserves you need to keep going. They are unique to every individual. Maybe it's a weekly church service; maybe it's a morning in the pedicure chair; maybe it's a golf game; maybe it's a lunch with a dear friend; maybe it's a dance lesson; or maybe it's just the luxury of a three-hour sitter so you can read a book! I don't know what will fill up your gas tank. What I do know is that you must find reserve energy. I believe this unrecognized need derails more caregivers than anything else. This is where low self-esteem and self-pity can sneak into your psyche. This is where you either want to give up or give in to destructive habits like addiction, abuse, long-term anger, or bitter resentment.

It's really quite simple but not easy to make sure you fill up your spiritual tank. Take charge of you. You would no more expect your car to take you to work when the tank is registering empty than you would fly to the moon. Find your renewables and pursue them with regularity.

Chapter 30

Waiting for the Prognosis

Caregiving often calls us to lean into love we didn't know possible.

—**Tia Walker,** *The Inspired Caregiver: Finding Joy While Caring for Those You Love*

At the beginning of this book, I shared that the initial prognosis for my mother was that she had only thirty days to live. Month one turned into month two, month two turned into month three, and so it went. As days turned into many months, I found myself overwhelmed with an odd sense of guilt. I wondered, "Is Mother going to die? And if so, when?" My commitment to bring her home with me was based largely on this short-term prognosis. It was an ambivalent feeling to be expecting the end to come and yet being glad that it had not. I had truly put my life on hold and could not make any plans for the future. I was in limbo.

It's not easy to admit to this ambivalence. Certainly I cherished every day Mother was alive, but I also saw how compromised her happiness became. I watched her deteriorate before my eyes. Her personal dignity was gone, and her independence was gone. She was ready to leave this earth and yet I still had to cheer her on—not to mention I had to cheer myself on. It was mentally exhausting. I wondered every night how much longer she had. I tried to make the best of every day though I'm quite sure I fell short. I tried to remember these wonderful words from Charles Dickens: "Have a heart that never hardens, and a temper that never tires, and a touch that never hurts."

Chapter 31

Second-Guessing Yourself

Not everyone will understand your journey. That's fine. It's not their journey to make sense of. It's yours.

—Zero Dean

t some point along your caregiving journey, you will second-guess yourself with lots of shouldas, wouldas, and couldas:

Why did I ever think I could do this?

Why don't my friends understand what I'm going through?

Why does my sister question every decision I make?

I should have been a better daughter or son.

I should be a better wife, mother, husband, or dad.

I could have been more loving and kind.

I would have done this so differently if I'd only known the future.

I could have been less pissy, more patient, and less depressed.

On and on it goes until you drive yourself mad. This is wasted energy when you are already low on fuel. It's your journey. Don't fall prey to reacting to criticism, judgment, second-guessing, or suggestions that don't work for you. It's your journey, darn it, so own it and get through it with your head held high. No one else offered to do what you're doing, and they probably could not do it any better. Believe it!

Chapter 32

The Smells

Each day has a color, a smell.
—**Chitra Banerjee Divakaruni,** *The Mistress of Spices*

In the short story I wrote while caring for Mother, I addressed the smells associated with dying: "Her house smelled of death to come, stale urine, dried blood, old clothes, and too much Lysol spray." These were not unlike the smells of a nursing home. If you have not ever visited one, you should. Your home will take on some of these odors no matter what you do. Mine was never *that* offensive but it was still depressing.

I'm a meticulous housekeeper but even I could not remedy the smells. Honestly, I'm not sure that I even wanted to. Somehow they were a part of this phase of life and validated the experience in my warped perspective. Everything was off-kilter.

My suggestion is to make this better by using diffusers, candles, plug-in air fresheners and anything else you can find. In the warmer months, open some doors and windows and let in as much fresh air as possible. Use ceiling fans to keep the fresh air circulating. (Many times people are allergic to these various options, so check that out before you use them.) And don't forget to bake chocolate chip cookies a lot. Realtors swear that this aroma creates a sense of warmth and good feelings in a home more than anything else you can do. Try it out on your loved one.

Smells don't lie but you can cover them up, perhaps better than I did.

Chapter 33

Bringing Church to You

For where two or three are gathered in my name,
there am I among them.

—Matthew 18:20, *New American Standard Bible*

*M*other attended church with avid regularity all of her life. After she moved from her home of forty-plus years to live in my city, she attended church with me for a decade. Those are some of my fondest memories. Never in my adult life had I had someone to sit with in church until this time with Mother. It was so meaningful to me!

When she became sick, church was out of the question. I made sure that Mother was still receiving both her home church bulletin and the weekly bulletin from our current church. She relished receiving those in the mail and spent hours reading through all the news of both old friends and new.

I also made sure we found a credible televised service on Sunday mornings. There was one in particular that she really loved that originated out of the television station I managed.

The minister was not of our denomination, but he was a fine Christian and his message was "nondenominational." Ironically, the broadcast was called *Abundant Living.* For Mother, Sundays at 9:30 a.m. became her church, and it was one of the highlights of her week. I even invited the minister to visit her from time to time, which absolutely lifted her spirits.

If church is meaningful to your loved one, find a course of action like I did to keep them feeling connected to their spiritual path.

Chapter 34

Keeping the Spiritual Connection

Prayer is our humble answer to the inconceivable surprise of living.

—Abraham Joshua Heschel

Frequent visits from my associate pastor proved to be a joy to my mother. She became fast friends with this female pastor named Elise, who had been recently ordained into the ministry. She and Mother had long conversations, many laughs, and I'm sure some tears. They ended with prayers. She was a total blessing. I think Mother took her under her wing to talk about wisdom and commitment in one's spiritual life. I always left them alone to have personal sharing time.

Mother asked that this pastor be the one to do her memorial service at the assisted living facility where she eventually resided at the end. And she did a magnificent job! A small crowd gathered on that day to celebrate what Elise called the three G's of Mother's life: Godliness, gratitude,

71

and graciousness. This is how she characterized Mother so appropriately.

The service lasted only ten minutes but it was perfect. Mother would never have wanted a big show, just a quiet moment of truth and reflection. Because of the time spent with Mother, Elise knew just the right tone for the service.

Find a spiritual confidante for your loved one if they are open to that. Even folks who haven't been "churchy" may benefit from having the freedom to discuss their fears and concerns about dying with a spiritual adviser. I personally don't believe a family member is the one best suited for this role. Find a connection out in the community or bring in someone your loved one already knows and admires. When this person is asked to participate in or lead the memorial service, he or she can do so with insight and affection and convey a beautiful testament to the life of your loved one. Peace of soul will bring peace of mind and body for them, and undoubtedly this will spill over to more peaceful times for you.

Chapter 35

The Legal Particulars of Dying

The fear of death follows from the fear of life. A
man who lives fully is prepared to die at any time.

—Mark Twain

s hard as I try, I find that my two adult
children don't want to discuss the legalities
and particulars around my death. I have tried
to do all the "before" prep work so the "after" will be easier
for them. It's definitely not a sexy conversation but it is so
necessary. Please don't avoid this discussion when you are
caring for a loved one.

Find out if they have a will and where it is kept. Find out if
they have an advanced medical directive which clearly states
their wishes should they need life support. Know where that
is stored. Make sure you know the location, number, and
contents of their safe deposit box; make sure you have a key;
make sure you have signed the signature card allowing entry;
and make sure you have added your name to all of their
checking and savings accounts. If you are the executor of the
estate, have a lawyer explain exactly what this will require of

you. In one computer file or notebook, put all the financial information about bank accounts, life insurance policies, safe deposit boxes, and keys as well as investment firms. Get names, locations, account numbers, and phone numbers.

Write up an obituary with your loved one so they can have some input. Believe it or not, it can be a fun experience working on it together, and it will take up one of those gray afternoons. Be prepared with burial plots or cremation procedures, and get as much of that purchased as you possibly can prior to the death event.

At the time of death, be prepared to obtain at least twenty death certificates, because you will need them to cover all the issues surrounding the legal ending of a life from social security to Medicare to pensions. People require proof, especially these days; just a phone call does not suffice. You can usually obtain death certificates from your local Health Department or through the Bureau of Vital Statistics at your state capital. Here in my community the cost is nominal: fifteen dollars for the first copy and six dollars for any thereafter. It's better and less expensive to have too many than not enough, as surprise situations will continue to come up several months after the death of your loved one.

I am forever amazed at really smart folks who don't take care of these particulars. Don't be one of the foolish ones. At the time of your loved one's death, you will be addled, grief-stricken, overwhelmed, and busy. Have all of this done before the fact.

Consider me weird or a bit morbid if you must, but consider me wise. Go forth and do the same!

Chapter 36

The Caregivers in Your Family

Example is not the main thing in influencing others. It is the only thing.

—Albert Schweitzer

*S*urely our caregiving ability is subtly determined by what we have observed and absorbed from family and even friends. My parents lived many hours from their families for most of their married lives. Thus, for me there was never any day-to-day caregiving in our home.

However, I have always been inspired by my aunt who took daily, tender care of my paternal grandmother. Every summer I spent at least a month with them in their tiny east Tennessee home. Early on, before my grandmother aged so much, I remember working in their garden, making homemade ice cream, and picking blackberries to make jam and cucumbers to make pickles. I remember jaunts to the county fair where Grandmother's rhubarb pie always took a first-place blue ribbon.

As the years went by, my spinster aunt tended to all of my grandmother's needs. It had to be a lonely, hard journey for her. From afar we never worried because we knew there was no reason. Not to say that all was perfect or without some "cussin' and yellin'" between them, which I always found hilarious, but my aunt did what she needed to do. I always remembered that and respected her so much. My aunt willingly gave up her life for my grandmother.

Maybe there's a kind word needed here for those of you who have to endure the caregiving process from a long distance. Surely this must also be soul-wrenching. Perhaps the most useful contribution you can make is to support, support, and support. Try to keep the criticism to a low murmur. Send up many prayers, cards, and occasionally even little gifts to your brother or sister or whomever is carrying the brunt of the load. Take a weekend shift if you possibly can and give them a break. Or commit your vacation to helping out so they can have a long respite to refuel. No doubt your guilt eats away at you, but stop that! If you were close at hand, you would do exactly what they are doing.

On the flip side, perhaps you have watched horrible situations arise in your family, where caregiving was cruel, unloving, or even abusive. Break that cycle even if you have to go for some counseling. Start afresh because your children are watching and subtly recording your daily example.

Caregiving comes in all colors and all shapes and sizes, but the end result must be tenderness and respect, however you manage to package it.

Chapter 37

A Visit from the Hairdresser

I think that the most important thing a woman can have—next to talent, of course—is her hairdresser.

—Joan Crawford

My mother was not vain but she did always like to look as nice as she could. She was by no means ever a fashion statement, but she was neat and stylish to the extent that her pocketbook would allow. However, she was never able to do her own hair (or mine!), and from the time I was a little girl, we always went regularly to the hairdresser. It was not a fine shop but the back of someone's house—you know the kind.

Several times when Mother was so very sick and could no longer get out, I had my hairdresser of thirty years come to the house to give her a haircut and style. We put her in the master bathroom in her wheelchair and turned it into a salon for a couple of hours. We laughed and chatted and had some good "girl" time. It was a real boost to Mother, because even though sick, old, and dying, she still had a healthy touch of vanity. It was great to see her look like her usual self.

There was a hidden motive here. In the back of my mind I knew the day would come when funerals would have to be arranged. That meant her body would have to be prepared. In tribute to Mother's vanity, I had my hairdresser come while Mother was able to offer feedback on how she typically wore her hair. This same hairdresser offered to do Mother's hair after she passed. That was a special favor and one of those kind gestures that you never forget. Mother looked absolutely beautiful, and her hair was just like she would have wanted.

Consider a plan to bring dignity to your loved one, even at their death.

Chapter 38

Spills, Stains, and
Overflowing Showers

I've learned that people will forget what you said,
people will forget what you did, but people will
never forget how you made them feel.

—Maya Angelou

ay after day I accumulated stains all over
my house: stains on the carpet, stains on
the upholstery from unintended spills, and
splatters on walls from unmentionable accidents. Some were
horrifying for me and some were just casual incidents. Most
humiliated my mother.

The shower was another issue to be sure. Usually a home
heath person came to assist Mother with this venture, but
it was pretty routine to have a flood on the bathroom floor
each time. The shower door had to be left open during the
entire process. It was just part of the ritual which meant
sopping up all the water with clean towels, washing all the
towels, drying all the towels, and then folding and putting

them away, knowing that you would go through these same motions almost every day.

It was hard. In some cases I waited until Mother moved from my house to remedy the issues. I really, really tried to act like none of it bothered me, but occasionally I would lose it and hateful, resentful diatribes would roll out of my mouth. How much I regret that now. It's so similar to memories of blow-ups with my children when they were little. Just as they looked on with sad eyes and broken hearts, so did Mother.

Carpets can be cleaned and walls can be painted. Chairs can be recovered. Floors can be mopped up. But all of this chaos is happening against a difficult setting. The real situation is that you are stretched and pulled; you are tired and trying; you are beyond your tolerance point—and suddenly there is the scene where you break. It's just so very hard. You try to grit your teeth and smile. Some days you will be proud of yourself; other days you will cry yourself to sleep.

Chapter 39

Unwanted Company from the Black Sheep of the Family

After all, the wool of a black sheep is just as warm.

—Ernest Lehman, *The Sound of Music*

I suppose that every family has a black sheep. In our case, it was my mother's sister. From the time we were children, we knew there was something off about her. Her chosen lifestyle was not similar to ours, and my father especially had no respect for her. However, true to my mother's character, she never stopped loving her sister and always made time to support and listen to her.

While Mother was sick, my aunt chatted with Mother almost every week by telephone.

It was a strange relationship to me because I had no time or use for the woman. What I came to understand, however, was a deep respect for Mother's love toward her only female sibling. (She had six brothers, all deceased. Mother was the oldest and practically raised the other seven. She told me that she was pretty much always a mother.)

One morning I was getting makeup on and hair dried when I heard an unexpected doorbell about 8:30. I threw on some clothes and rushed to the door. There stood not only my aunt but also her daughter and son-in-law who had driven four hours from Tennessee to visit. I was so aggravated that they had not called ahead to let us know. This was so typical on their part.

But Mother lit up like a Christmas tree, welcoming them all in for a long visit. Mother was gracious, kind, and hospitable. I was aloof and probably obviously irritated that they had come. It was just one more stress point that I didn't need.

How wrong I was! It was Mother's company to host, not mine. It was one of those regrettable moments. Try to accept the black sheep of the family and the warmth they may bring to your loved one.

Chapter 40

9/11

For me and my family personally, September 11 was a reminder that life is fleeting, impermanent, and uncertain. Therefore, we must make use of every moment and nurture it with affection, tenderness, beauty, creativity, and laughter.

—Deepak Chopra

A prearranged vacation out of the country separated me from Mother for two weeks. I had made, as you can imagine, a million scheduled details to cover my absence. My sister and her husband stayed at my house and took over the day-to-day care, but I had set up the overnight sitters and all the hospice folks. I needed a break!

Unbelievably, the span of travel time was the first two weeks of September 2011. Yes, that means that I was out of the country on the tragic day the Twin Towers were attacked. It was a surreal experience from every possible angle. We were in Vienna, Austria, and I heard about the attack after dinner that evening. Our hearts were broken and we felt totally disconnected from the events at home. Our hotel television did not have a single channel in English, but the pictures were message enough. At the Swiss embassy the next morning, we walked over to sign their visitors' log, along with hundreds of others who had come to pay their respects. Later we each received a personal letter of condolence from the Austrian Director of Tourism.

We took a bus to Prague later in the day, where people lined the streets with memorials to the victims, many coming up to us crying and offering their condolences—and in a language we did not know. The body language of grief needs no translation.

It was an experience I will never forget. Mother was devastated, worried, and very glad when I made it back home. I caught the first flight permitted to leave for the United States out of Paris.

My first task when I returned was to put an American flag in our window. I missed the emotional connection of a nation in mourning, which I will always regret. Mother had a few days where the focus was totally off her illness and she could embrace a wider grief than her own.

Chapter 41

Adult Children

What we desire our children to become, we must
endeavor to be before them.

—Andrew Combe

I dedicate this meditation to my adult son and
his wife. At the time Mother was sick, they
were still relatively newly married and had no
children. Most Friday's, after working all week, they drove
two hours to give up their weekend so I could have some
rest. They were both trained as nurses and understood
exactly what to do and how to care for Mother. She adored
having the nice break. She and I grew tired of each other as
you can imagine.

My son and his wife insisted that I go out, relax, connect
with friends, or go to a movie. They cooked and assisted in
every possible way, some not so pleasant. They are the ones
who showed me how to lift Mother from her wheelchair and
out of bed, so I would not hurt my back.

One day before the holidays, my son was the one who
straightforwardly said, "Mom, you can't do this anymore!"

He insisted that I start to think about other arrangements, as I was hurting my back and exhausted most of the time.

At those moments you realize that all you tried to do for your children comes back to you in loving doses. They supported me to the end, and I will never, ever forget it! I truly hope you are as lucky as I was with help from your adult children.

Chapter 42

A Taping Session

Speech is the voice of the heart.

—Anna Quindlen

Toward the end of Mother's stay at my house, I had an idea: I wanted Mother to make an audio tape for each of my children. My motivation was selfish. My dad died much too early, when he was only seventy-two, and I can hardly remember the sound of his voice. I yearn to hear it one more time. I wanted to preserve Mother's voice for my children so they would never forget it.

I worked with Mother for days, writing down memories of times together with my kids: births, holidays, summer vacations, trips, even times when they were little snits! We worked on this for days because she would get tired, and then we'd lay it aside and start again on another day.

I typed the words all out for her and had her practice without me in the room. Her voice was shaky and weak, but she finally got excited about doing this, as long as we took our time.

Then the big day came where we tried the first recording on a small tape recorder that she had given me. Technology has really changed! We used those tiny little cassette tapes in a recorder that was probably three inches by four inches; it was easy for her to hold. I reassured her that there was no reason to stress, as we could erase and rerecord as many times as needed until it was exactly how she wanted it.

This became a loving project and gave Mother something to look forward to for about three weeks. I'm so glad we did it. I gave both my son and my daughter their personalized version set to the tone of their lives. I hope they still have the tapes and listen to them occasionally. I'm afraid to ask them.

This might be a great project for you depending on the strength and attitude of your loved one. And by the way, make a copy for yourself. I didn't think to do that and I'm so sorry now!

Chapter 43

Sharing Memories

Nothing is ever really lost to us as long as we remember it.

—**L.M. Montgomery,** *The Story Girl*

ometimes, we get so involved in the day-to-day caregiving cycle that we forget what an opportunity the time affords us with a loved one. I encourage you to spend an hour every day rummaging back through old scrapbooks and pictures, treasures that have been kept about the family. Journey down memory lane together. You might find some amazing discoveries, as I did.

Mother shared with me that she never wanted children as a young, married adult because, as she said, "I have been a mother all of my life." She was the oldest of eight children and was always expected to care for her younger siblings. She shyly confided in me that she hated Sunday afternoons when she was growing up because her mother and daddy "hid" in their bedroom with the door locked, leaving Mother in charge. Many times after that, there was another baby. She didn't quite understand as a young girl, but of course she eventually figured it out!

Mother also told me that she married my dad to get away from her home life, only to discover how wonderful being in relationship with him was for her. She never knew that marriage could be so happy. What a fantastic thing to share. She also told me that moving to Huntsville and leaving her home of forty-two years after Daddy died was horrific for her because she thought he didn't know where she was. One day she had a dream, and in the dream Daddy was standing in her new apartment kitchen at the stove, frying eggs. She was elated because he had found her. After that she was able to embrace the move and be at peace.

I hope this suggestion will prove very meaningful for you. Ask questions that you've always wanted to ask like, "What was really wrong with _____?" (fill in the blank) or "Why did you do this, or why didn't you do that?" Write some of this down and update the family Bible with names, dates, births, deaths, etc. It will be your last chance to share in true intimacy. Take gentle advantage of it.

Embracing
Change

Chapter 44

Giving Up and Moving to Assisted Living

You are doomed to make choices. This is life's greatest paradox.

—Wayne Dyer, *Mind Secret Blog*

The decision to move Mother to an assisted living facility right down the street was difficult for everyone. It was an admission for me of inadequacy, of not being able to live up to my commitment to care for her. With my sister, it was one of those sibling confusions where she felt left out of the decision despite a letter I wrote to her explaining all of my reasons.

But the hardest blow was to my mother. She never said a word of complaint to me, but I knew that it hurt and disappointed her terribly. I think she felt like I had cast her to the wind with strange people and possibly inadequate care. As it turned out, the care was excellent, but her fears were monumental, much like those of a small child.

I had withdrawal for the first week and was at the facility almost around the clock. God was on our side the first night, as she was assigned a fantastic attendant who checked on her every hour, which lessened Mother's fears. This woman had no idea what a godsend she was.

Slowly, as the days went by, Mother acclimated as she always did. She was never in love with the place, but I think she saw that it was a necessary step. She had watched me grow tired and weary. With time there was for her a sense of relief that she was feeling less like a burden.

I went by the assisted living facility every morning and every evening and many times ate the evening meal with Mother. The atmosphere was depressing because so many were worse off than she was—too many wheelchairs, walkers, oxygen tanks, and yes, too many smells!

I made the best of it. Mother spent her time thanking everyone for their assistance, and they adored her! Surely you're not surprised.

Chapter 45

Smaller Spaces

The secret of happiness, you see, is not found in seeking more, but in developing the capacity to enjoy less.

—Socrates

other had trouble adjusting at first to the very tiny space at the assisted living facility. Her bedroom was also the sitting area, which was also the mini kitchen—all one in the same. I'd guess it was 250 square feet at most. There was an accessible bathroom large enough for her wheelchair and a walk-in shower. The "kitchen" had a tiny bar sink and a small microwave. The design was intentional to discourage cooking in the rooms, which was ultimately a smart idea. My sister bought her a new twin bed that was so much better than the hospital bed in my home, and that was a smile-pleasing plus for her.

Mother's meals were provided either in her room or in a nice dining area, but she did not know a soul. Imagine starting all over at age eighty-two and learning all new friends. It is not an easy situation for anyone of any age.

Growing old and giving up your possessions is not for the weak hearted. First for Mother, it had been the selling of her house of twenty-five years, and then it was the move to an apartment in Huntsville. This was followed by the move to independent living, which meant giving up over half of her furniture, etc. Next it was moving into my house, where her things were in storage, and finally it was the move to the assisted living facility, where she lost almost everything. She had only her Bible, her television, a bed, her recliner, one side chair for visitors, her toiletries, and a few dishes and a coffee pot. That's not much to represent such a full life.

But Mother had the same heart and keen mind as always and was ever the gentle spirit. Those things could not be taken away! Not once did she complain, and she made the best of every day. She went to the social times and concerts; she went to play cards and hear lectures. She gave it her very best shot. She had to be lonely and brokenhearted, but she never once let me know. Her face broke into a big smile every time I rounded the door into her tiny room.

Chapter 46

Learning to Trust All Over Again

> None of us knows what might happen even the
> next minute, yet still we go forward. Because we
> trust. Because we have Faith.
>
> **—Paulo Coelho,** *Brida*

Suddenly with the move to assisted living, there were more strangers in our lives. There were new people all around, some more pleasant than others, some more tender than others. I was friends with Laurie, the director, prior to placing Mother in this facility, and that became a great connection. It always pays to have friends in high places, as the saying goes.

Laurie was a feisty, caring individual who made Mother her project. She ran a tight, efficient ship and worked ridiculous hours to keep the assisted living facility one of the best around. She went by almost daily to check on Mother and would sit and listen and hold her hand. Voila! Mother adored Laurie, and this more than anything helped with the transition. Slowly we all learned to trust the process.

Even my sister and her husband saw Laurie as a huge plus, which made my life much easier. They still came over twice a week and now had a place to sit and relax out in the comfortable waiting area. They could visit with Mother without feeling that they were imposing on my home and private space. It really turned out to be a great arrangement for all of us—at least on the surface.

Mother made a few friends and had her eighty-third birthday while living there, as I've already shared. It was the best of a difficult situation.

Check out your assisted living facilities well in advance of making a move. Some are more credible than others. With the Internet, Facebook, and Twitter, you can do a darn good job of getting down to the real truths about patient care. No place will be perfect, but you can feel more confident with a good report card. Get a personal reference from someone who has gone before you with a loved one.

I salute all of those who work in these kinds of facilities day after day with relatively low wages. They all deserve a special place in heaven.

Chapter 47

The Importance of a Vacuum Cleaner

Little things console us because little things afflict us.

—Blaise Pascal

I am frequently amazed how much a small gesture can mean when times are tough and people are stretched to the maximum level of their mental tolerance and physical stamina. Such was the case with a simple vacuum cleaner.

My mother (like me) was an immaculate housekeeper. And yet in her present state, she could not perform any of her usual daily chores. She couldn't make her own bed, wash dishes, vacuum, or dust her living space, or even get herself bathed and dressed. She just sat all day and thought about her dysfunction. She sat and looked around at dust and clutter. She sat and wished to "ret up," as she called it, that daily run-through in a house where everything is quickly put in order. Imagine just sitting without the ability to do anything. Mother was still so sharp mentally that nothing escaped her—no thread on the carpet, speck of dust, or dirty dish! I can only imagine that this inertia was maddening for her.

Mother's space was cleaned several times a week by the maintenance folks but not to Mother's standards. So every day I would get her little vacuum cleaner and feather duster and make a quick sweep of the one room which she occupied. That made all the difference for her. She always felt together after that and able to move into her day. It took maybe five minutes for me but gave her a day's worth of mental ease. It sounds kind of silly, but I understood perfectly.

For the same reasons (even though laundry service was provided), I always took her clothes home with me to wash, which she much preferred. It was a good system and brought her a sense of calm.

The positive impacts of small gestures are never forgotten—otherwise, I wouldn't be writing about a vacuum cleaner!

Chapter 48

The Fall

The sensation of falling was the worst part.
—**Cassandra Clare,** *City of Bones*

One morning I popped in on Mother early in the day only to find a terrible situation. She was sitting calmly in her recliner, waiting on me like always. But what I saw broke my heart. She had fallen during the prior evening, and her face and nose had taken the brunt of the fall. Her face was black and she had broken her glasses. When I looked at her and gasped, she started to cry. Then she said the words I will never forget: "I'm so sorry! Please don't be mad at me." I replied, "Mother, why in the world do you think I would be mad at you?!" This was her mindset of not wanting to be a burden. She continued on and on with her regret of adding to my worry and told me that she would be more careful.

Truth be known, she had gotten out of bed during the night and tried to get into her wheelchair without assistance. I had made her promise me that she would not do that. Thus, she felt guilt and remorse. We had a long talk and revisited why she had to ask for help, but this episode reinforced the new state of affairs: I was the parent and she was the child. When I left her, I cried all the way home.

Avoid the temptation to belittle when accidents happen, even when your loved one knows they did something they weren't supposed to do. A hug is what they need more than a reprimand.

Chapter 49

Sunday Afternoons

I hate Sunday afternoons!
They are the loneliest time of the week,
The epitome of isolation
when your heart is bleak.

For years, it's been my hardest day.
The idle hours, the sense of loss,
The yearning for connection
Like a stone which has no moss.

—Linda Spalla

*S*unday afternoons in an assisted living facility are the worst. They are the loneliest, the hardest to get through. We all expect "something" from Sundays, I think; when there's only emptiness, it carves a hollow spot in your soul.

In fact, Sundays had been the pits for me for a very long time. When you are single, as I was, it's the disjointed day of the week where most are connected with family or just chilling in their home environment. Finding something or someone to occupy Sunday afternoons was the hardest work I did all week. (I have learned to enjoy just being alone, but it's taken many years.)

I would go over early to visit Mother and watch her television church with her, read the newspaper, and then stay around for lunch in the dining area. If the weather was somewhat nice, we would load up in her wheelchair and go for a spin outside. It was very difficult pushing her up and down a bumpy path, but we made the best of it and took advantage of warm breezes and sunshine on our faces. She loved that part of it. On cold afternoons, I would ask for help in getting her into the car, and we would just ride, mostly the country roads or out to new subdivisions to look at new houses. I tried to keep her in the warmth of the sunshine as much as I could.

In the pit of my stomach was always a hollow emptiness. Here we were, two lonely folks without much of a purpose, hanging on to each other as a means to form our day. I wish we had talked more.

Chapter 50

Continue with Celebrations

There is still no cure for the common birthday.

—John Glenn

During the time I cared for Mother, she had her eighty-third birthday, and we had a little party. By that time she was in assisted living, but we did the whole enchilada with balloons, cake, party favors, and games. The other residents and a few friends and family attended. Mother was truly not feeling well by then, but she presented her best side. She was gracious, as always, smiled and laughed, and thanked everyone for coming. In some ways, it was surreal for me, and I wondered why I was going through these motions. But it seemed the right thing to do. Mother knew it was her last and final birthday, and so did I.

The celebration was a way to say "I love you" even when circumstances were terrible and to show that life moves on even when you're not ready for it. Mother thanked me profusely but couldn't wait for everyone to leave.

I'm glad I had the party because Mother died two months later. Continue to celebrate birthdays with your loved ones. Realistically they are not as jubilant perhaps, but they still count in the heart and rank up there with being all you can be as a devoted caregiver.

The End and
the Beginning

Chapter 51

The Dreaded Call

Of all the wonders that I yet have heard,
It seems to me most strange that men should fear;
Seeing that death, a necessary end,
Will come when it will come.

—William Shakespeare, *Julius Caesar*

At 5:02 a.m. on April 12, 2002, I received the dreaded phone call. I knew the second my phone rang so early in the morning what the message would be. Mother had died during the night and been found by one of the attendants. I threw on some clothes and rushed to the assisted living facility which was only three minutes from my house.

Laurie, the director and my friend, was already there with tears running down her face. She and I had a private moment to sit, and I was able to touch Mother, now cold and stiff, and say "Good-bye" and "I love you." That was hard, very hard, but I'm glad I had a moment before the deluge of people started coming into the room: hospice came to prepare the body for being moved; a doctor came to pronounce her officially dead;

her favorite sitter, Sally, had asked to be called; and finally the ambulance came to transport her to the funeral home. It's still a blur. Then my sister came with her husband, and we went over all the prearranged plans.

After that I remember just going home, like a lost puppy without its mother. I sat for a while with that horrible sense of ambivalence. I was grief-stricken at losing Mother but so glad that she was now at rest. Her pain and discomfort had been growing with each passing day. I remember thinking how glad she would be to see my daddy and what a reunion they would have.

It's truly hard to know how to feel. I have the "do what you have to do" gene, and I slowly got up and did all that I was supposed to do. So will you.

Chapter 52

A Wish Come True

Sometimes things become possible if we want them bad enough.

—T.S. Eliot

All through the days and months of Mother's illness, she had prayed to die in her sleep, without any great pain or fuss. This was so Mother! It's a wish that many of us desire.

Just as she wanted, Mother did die peacefully in her sleep. She never called for help during the night, as far as we know, and I need to believe that she had no pain. She simply drifted into a peaceful calm in perfect accord with her life. What a blessing for her and for all around her. God is definitely good.

Facing Death

Facing death in the eye
is the longest day of my life;
the saddest moan of my soul;
the scariest emptiness I've ever known.

She is the world to me:
the basis, the start, the scope,
the inner workings, the desires,
the regrets, the standards;
the absolute pure benchmark
by which I have measured life.

Without her, my gauge will be missing.
Without her, my strength will be less.
My vision will be narrowed,
but my memories ...
reassuredly warm and blessed.

Facing life without her,
my mother dear,
will intensify all that she has been,
all that she has shared,
all that I hope to embrace.
She is the best the world can make.

                                        Linda Spalla

Chapter 53

Her Glasses

People see only what they are prepared to see.
—Ralph Waldo Emerson

held Mother's viewing in Huntsville so local friends could stop by to pay their final respects. On that day I was most definitely living on fumes. There was so much to be done: last-minute arrangements at the funeral home, the last viewing with family, greeting friends, enduring grief, and trying to be normal. It all required so much strength and courage. Having spent most of my life alone, I knew that my final good-bye to Mother before closing her casket would be done by myself.

I watched as everyone else in the family said their good-byes. Then I slowly made my way up to the casket for just a quiet moment. I took my time; I noticed how nice she looked, especially her hair, and silently thanked my hairdresser once again for such an act of kindness. I noticed her dress, the one that she had worn at my son's wedding several years back. It was one of her favorites. I noticed her gentle hands and manicured nails. I noticed the peacefulness of her face, not a smile but almost.

Suddenly without a thought of prior planning, I reached over and gently removed her glasses from her face. They seemed to be luring me. I wanted something of her to keep forever. They had touched her body, been her constant companion every day, and I wanted to have them as a special keepsake. My dad's hat and my mother's glasses now sit side by side on a bookcase in my bedroom, sacred ground for me.

I hope you will take your time and do what feels appropriate for you in the midst of these suspended circumstances. So often final moments become a blur. Try to focus and remember. You will be proud afterward that you persisted in staying in the moment.

Chapter 54

The Funeral

Death is not extinguishing the light; it is putting
out the lamp because dawn has come.

—Rabindranath Tagore

Mother resided in another city (two hours away) for more than forty years. My father was buried there and their burial plots were side by side. After the memorial service in my city, we made arrangements to get her body buried in her hometown the next day. The funeral was held in the chapel of her home church, which was the church of my youth.

I watched on that beautiful sunshine day (thank you, God) as Mother's remaining friends slowly made their way into the service. These were folks I knew when I was a child; now they were old and frail. It was on the one hand sad but also exhilarating.

Mother and I had gone over the funeral service many times, and all was as she wanted it. The minister read one of my poems entitled, "My Angel, My Mother."

The graveside service went quickly. Following that, the dear sweet friends from church had prepared lunch for all of us. Mother loved these people, and it was so appropriate to have them spreading joy and laughter along with great food. Mother would have been pleased. My children were very supportive, but then everyone left to resume their lives.

The long drive home was numbing for me. I was exhausted and suddenly it sank in—the grief, the sadness, the ambivalence, the stark awareness of change. Driving is very good think time, and I remained in total silence in my car with no music or blaring radio. It was just myself and my thoughts, some tears and the beginnings of learning to live without my mother.

Please don't wait until the reality of death to plan your loved one's funeral. You will be overwhelmed. Have the details covered to the extent you can. It's not a time for family disagreements and tension. It's not a time to stretch your capacity beyond where it is already stretched. Even with much prior planning, it will still be hectic and busy. If you can find a quiet moment alone to collect your thoughts before you leave for the funeral, you will be glad. This is the final good-bye, and you want to be as aware and present as you can possibly be.

Chapter 55

Relief

Your grief is as personal and unique as your fingerprint; no one else will have the same bereavement experience as you and there is not one "correct" way to respond to loss.

—Dr. Therese A. Rando

We've all said the adage, "Time heals all wounds." I hate to hear that, and I hate more to say it, but it is absolutely true. The days right after Mother's death were the hardest. There was a finality and sadness in cleaning out her room, packing up her few possessions and her clothes, but I had done so much of that already. She had downsized in many stages. There were days of many tears. Then, slowly, as time passed, my life took on more of its usual tempo, and a huge sense of relief came over me.

Most of all, I knew that I was at peace with my caregiving effort. I knew Mother was happy in heaven. I had no more sitters, no more strangers in my house. I had carpets cleaned and walls repainted. I had no one relying on me for anything.

I began to relax and sleep. The days went slowly at first but soon began to pass by in triple time. I had lost ground to make up with friends, community commitments to reengage in, golf to play, and travels to plan.

I knew Mother was watching and smiling because she more than anyone would be happy to see me back to my usual routine and "normal" life. She was not in pain any longer and had no sense of being a burden to me. That was worth celebrating.

Let me be very clear, however. There is not a day that goes by that I do not talk to her. It's usually when I'm walking. I move her things around in my house with exquisite tenderness. I struggle when I give her things away, as I had to do when I moved recently, downsizing myself. I asked for her forgiveness as though she was right there in the room with me, and maybe she was.

Inside my jewelry box, on the left-hand front corner, I have a ringlet of her delicate white hair which the hairdresser gave me when she was doing Mother's hair at my house. I treasure that. It is a living piece of her and I will keep it forever. Hopefully you will find a personal item to represent your loved one that you can forever hold dear in a special spot known only to you.

Chapter 56

Getting Through It But Never Getting Over It

Joy comes, grief goes, we know not how.

—James Russell Lowell

After Mother passed away, my sister read about a grief seminar being held at one of our local hospitals. I was pleased that she wanted us to go together. I don't remember much except for one poignant thought. The facilitator differentiated between getting over the loss versus getting through it. Why, he said, would we ever want to "get over" the feelings and life we had with our loved one? What we wanted to work toward was just to "get though" the grief process. I liked that very much and have never forgotten it. It made perfectly good sense to my orderly brain.

I have never gotten over missing Mother or thinking of her. I still use all of her recipes preserved in her own handwriting. I use all of her remedies for colds and sore throats and stain removals. I try to pass these on to my children and grandchildren. I still make the very same Thanksgiving and

Christmas menus as she did, and her recipes for cornbread dressing and pecan pie are notorious in the family. I love to tell stories about her to my grandchildren, a bedtime ritual when we are together.

I have gotten through the grief process, as it has now been twelve years since Mother's passing. I have accomplished much and have a wonderful, full life. I do it all knowing how proud she was of me, how in awe she was of my accomplishments. No matter how dysfunctional my life became, she was always my greatest advocate.

The aftermath is the very best time to do some journaling. Writing your way through the deluge of feelings can move you along your recovery much faster. If that doesn't suit you, take up jogging or fishing, gardening or bird watching, something which you can do alone with moments of solitude and quietness. Our society doesn't afford much of this quiet time; you will have to make it. I call it simply processing time. You can make the best dough in the world, but if you don't let it sit for a while and process, it will not rise into the light, fluffy bread you desire.

Chapter 57

Recycling the Leftovers

We are not to throw away those things which can benefit our neighbor. Goods are called good because they can be used for good; they are instruments for good, in the hands of those who use them properly.

—Clement of Alexandria, Christian theologian

*A*t the end of this journey, you will have some leftovers, some items you no longer need, things like wheelchairs, walkers, bedside commodes, walking canes, adult diapers, and pee pads. I even had multiple cans of Ensure that Mother never consumed. These are tough reminders, so I suggest that you devise a way to recycle them quickly. You may have rented many of these items, and if so, good for you. It's just a day's work to return them, and you are done.

I didn't go that route, so I had some decisions to make. I chose to keep the large items for possible future use, either by myself or my sister. My sister had bought much of it, and they were really not mine to dispose of. So I very carefully wrapped each article in strong plastic bags and stored them in my garage. As it turned out, my sister was able to use most everything when she became ill.

Other good options are to give items both large and small to your local non-profit hospice, to organizations like Purple Heart or Wounded Warrior, or to your local homeless shelter or community free clinic. Naturally, some will be more eager to get these than others if they are used. But for goodness sake, recycle as much as you can. Don't flush the leftover medicines down the toilet or allow them to get into the water system. Find out on the Internet who in your community will dispose of them for you.

It helps to close the final chapter by getting all of these reminders out of your sight. Recycling reinforces the depth of your love by sharing them with those in need.

Chapter 58

Flying Solo

My emotions overload because there is no hand to hold, there's no shoulder here to lean on; I'm walking all on my own.

—Christina Aguilera, "The Right Man"

Many of you reading this book will be divorced like me—some twice divorced like me. It doesn't make us bad people. It means we had bad luck, were victims of fate or circumstance, had bad timing, or made poor choices. No one in his or her right mind sets out to become divorced. I contend if people who divorce really knew what lay ahead, the divorce rate would plummet.

What people don't realize is that divorce has far-reaching ramifications. Not only do you live and parent alone, you also spend many weekends and holidays alone. You travel alone; you sit in church alone; you go to the movies alone. What no one considers is that you also grandparent alone and, alas, caregive alone. This means double the work and double the responsibility. There is no partner to share the physical load or the mental struggle. There is no extra set of hands to give you a break or to lift something or to run an errand. It's just you.

Depending on how well you know yourself, make sure you are up for the challenge of flying solo with your caregiving. Know not only your physical strength but your mental well-being. It's a daunting task. Don't take it on because you think you should. Take it on because you know you can.

Chapter 59

How to Be When It's Over

Don't go through life, *grow* through life.

—Eric Butterworth

*S*uddenly you wake up after the funeral and you are no longer a caregiver. It's a bit of a shock to your system. You resume your old life but with some reflection and most likely with a big emotional hole in your world. "What do I do with myself now?" you ask. You may catch yourself reverting back to old patterns and old habits and then suddenly realizing that you don't have to do any of that anymore. It's a strange feeling. I've never lost a baby, but I can only imagine that this transition might be like having a miscarriage. One day you are totally caught up in being pregnant; the next day you are not.

Be prepared for a sense of not only sadness but isolation, along with the relief that you're not quite able to celebrate yet. You can take your long walks again or have lunch with a friend or hit the golf course at whatever hour you please. Part of you wants to jump and shout at the freedom, but it seems somehow irreverent. It's really not, and you should try letting yourself celebrate. You did your very best. You weren't perfect but better than most, *n'est-ce pas*? Life does move on, and you have to move on with it.

You've had a unique privilege. You've been able to find a growth spot in your life as an adult. Long after your body has grown to its full physical potential, you've had the chance to grow mentally and emotionally. Try framing your journey this way and your healing process will be much less sad. It just might be the most enriching time of your life!

Chapter 60

Getting Used to the Aftershocks

I get mail; therefore I am.

—Scott Adams

*T*have always loved to get mail, real mail from the post office. Something about being remembered, the connection, the unexpected—I'm not sure what the fascination is for me, but it's always been the high spot of my day. I never miss checking my mail and stand in amazement at folks who let days, even weeks, pass without checking.

After Mother's death, the trip to the mailbox became less enjoyable, however. Because she had moved her official residence to mine and changed her mailing address, I received all of her mail for the eight months she was with me. Suddenly, after her death, I was never ready for the punch in the stomach when I opened the box to see mail addressed to her. It took months to send out notices of her death with the polite request that she be removed from mailing lists. It was cold and business-like but necessary; I hated it. One day someone's life is full and vibrant; the next, their existence is a deletion. It was a part of the grief process that I never anticipated. It's just one of those steps you have to endure to know about—like labor pains, I suppose.

The worst slaps in the face were those from folks who should have known better, who let Mother's death slip through the cracks. For example, my church directory, published months after her death, still had her listed but (thank God) without a picture. Her own church in her home of forty years continued to send the weekly bulletin until I called to inform them. Anyone that she had ever made a donation to continued to query her for money. On and on it went for at least a year until finally the mail addressed to her stopped. I thought I would be glad, but then sometimes I missed seeing her name on the envelope. I was surprised at my own ambivalence and suspect that you will be also. Something about seeing her name still there eased the finality of death. As the above quotation says so poignantly, "I get mail; therefore I am."

Chapter 61

The Inheritance

Sometimes the poorest man leaves his children the richest inheritance.

—Ruth E. Renkel

*A*fter many weeks had passed, I discovered a letter from Mother's estate attorney in my mailbox. Much to my surprise, Mother had managed on a very meager income to put aside some savings. I was absolutely shocked to find an enclosed check for twenty thousand dollars. Given my family's socioeconomic status and financial struggles, this was like getting a check for $250,000. Remember that my sister had handled all of Mother's finances. Indeed, it was another punch in the stomach but of a totally different kind. I remember just falling to my knees and sitting down on the curb. The tears began to flow. The memories began to flood.

How much I remembered that Mother never bought herself a new winter coat so that my sister and I could have one as we were growing up, or that she used to hide the weekly box of cookies in a different place in the kitchen because they had to last the entire week—no money for extras. I never told my folks how much I wanted to go to Birmingham Southern College because I knew they couldn't afford it. I got my own college loan and paid it back for five years after graduating. With the passing years, Mother saw no need for new clothes and wore the same outfits over and over again. She derived no pleasure from shopping.

I was aghast at Mother's frugality as she had lived on pauper's wages of just her social security check, a meager twelve hundred dollars per month. How in the world had she accumulated twenty thousand dollars? And how in the world could I take her money? My mind was awhirl with a million thoughts and emotions. It absolutely wasted me that hot May afternoon.

With time, I came to understand the need to accept the gift as the act of love it was, and I set about to decide what to do with it. The hesitancy, regret, and guilt turned into celebration and joy. I wanted to use it very carefully in a way that would thrill her. My choices narrowed and the decision grew clearer: I decided to spend it on my daughter's upcoming August wedding, knowing how pleased Mother would be. It would position her right in the middle of the wedding festivities. I explained this to my own daughter, and she caught the specialness of the gesture.

I don't know if you will be lucky enough to get an inheritance from your loved one. If you do, no matter the amount, treasure the love message and spend it with care and fondness to celebrate their life.

Final Word:
Tie a Knot and Hang On

When you're at the end of your rope, tie a knot and hang on.

—One of Mother's favorite sayings

*S*ome of us are blessed to get what I call "the do what you have to do" gene. Whatever the circumstance, whatever puts us at the end of our rope, whatever tragedy or setback befalls us, some of us can tie a knot, hang tough, and figure out what to do. Caregiving requires a lot of that. Hanging on is all you will do some days. The courage to persist, the ability to start fresh every day, the belief that hope is around the corner—all of these represent good mental health. And caregiving will afford you more practice at this skill than you want.

However, there will be some more tying of knots after your loved one is gone. You will find yourself in search of a new normal. Time is truly the great healer, but the catch to that old adage is that you have to live through the moments, the days, the weeks, the months, yes, even the years until time has released its healing balm. You will undoubtedly have a few regrets, but I hope you have more of a sense of having spun a beautiful piece of your life's quilt.

In the aftermath, you will be changed forever: you will be emotionally stronger; you will be a better friend; you will be a better listener; you will be a better parent to your own children; you will be wistful and full of memories. You will no longer have to live on fumes. You will have learned to stop, catch your breath, and find the strength to do more than you ever imagined yourself capable of doing. You will find that despite all the struggles and challenges, the passage has been a defining moment. You will have become your best self!

Godspeed on your caregiving journey.

About the Author

*L*inda Spalla has been called a "steel magnolia in the flesh."[1] She achieved great success in a twenty-five-year corporate management career for the New York Times Company. Working her way up the ladder at WHNT-TV in Huntsville, Alabama, hers was a Cinderella story. Divorced, jobless, and homeless in 1975, she began her journey as a secretary and ended as the president and general manager of the CBS affiliate owned by the New York Times Company. She led the television station from third place to first place as general manager.

Linda was one of the first females in top corporate television management in the Deep South. She was also one of the few women managers among CBS affiliates, and the first woman selected for television management for the New York Times Broadcast Group. During this time, she was a wife, mother, daughter, and community enthusiast who never lost her femininity or her Southern roots.

Linda's first book entitled *Leading Ladies*, published in 2003, offers practical leadership tips for women. In *Bernie and Me ... A Paris Love Story*, Linda describes with tender and often humorous clarity her ten years visiting Paris with her

---

[1] Joyce Dixon, Southern Scribe Reviews www.southernscribe.com

best friend and lover, Bernard Verdier, a native Frenchman. From Southern belle to world traveler, she will delight you with her Parisian escapades and her love affair with Bernie. Hopefully she will inspire you to fall in love with Paris as she has. The book is due out in 2015.

In *Catch Your Breath*, Linda has written a raw, honest series of meditations for caregivers, based on her experiences in caring for her own mother. These meditations will evoke both laughter and tears as they offer insight and courage to those caught in the caregiving web.